Knockouts

The Bakerloo flea

LONGMAN GROUP LIMITED
Longman House,
Burnt Mill, Harlow, Essex CM20 2JE, England
and Associated Companies throughout the World.

This edition first published 1979
Second impression 1983

ISBN 0 582 20077 6

Printed in Hong Kong by
Hing Yip Printing Co.

Knockouts

Michael Rosen

THE BAKERLOO FLEA

drawings by Quentin Blake

Longman

Knockouts

General Editor: Josie Levine

The Salmon Ewart Alexander
Mia Gunnel Beckman
Mia Alone Gunnel Beckman
The Marco File Peter Buchanan
The Man Who Came Back Jan Carew
The Cat People Jan Carew
Save The Last Dance For Me and other stories Jan Carew
Stranger Than Tomorrow Jan Carew
The Bike Racers Bruce Carter
In The Beginning John Christopher
Three Plays Isobel D'Arcy
Love at a Bus Stop Janet Green
The Six Janet Green
The Six: Getting By Janet Green
The Six: Turning Points Janet Green
Behind the Goal John Griffin
Rumble Fish S. E. Hinton
Week Out Geraldine Kaye
A Northern Childhood: The Balaclava Story and other stories George Layton
A Northern Childhood: The Fib and other stories George Layton
Long Journey Home Julius Lester
The Job Margaret Loxton
Odysseus Returns Kenneth McLeish
The Robe of Blood and other stories Kenneth McLeish
The Bakerloo Flea Michael Rosen
Ginger Mick Joan Tate
Luke's Garden Joan Tate
The Runners Joan Tate
See You and other stories Joan Tate
You Can't Explain Everything Joan Tate
The Midwich Cuckoos John Wyndham

Picture Story Books: *Cave Rescue and other stories* Josie Levine

Cassette tapes, with readings from the books, are available for the following:

The Marco File read by Robert Powell
Save The Last Dance For Me read by Valentine Dyall
Stranger Than Tomorrow read by Edward Petherbridge
The Six read by Tony Robinson
The Six: Getting By read by Michael Burlington and Anthony Hyde
The Six: Turning Points read by David Goodland and Brian Hewlett
A Northern Childhood: The Balaclava Story and other stories read by George Layton
A Northern Childhood: The Fib and other stories read by George Layton
Long Journey Home read by Guy Gregory and Valerie Murray
Odysseus Returns read by Christian Rodska
The Robe of Blood read by Jill Balcon
The Bakerloo Flea read by Michael Rosen
You Can't Explain Everything read by Miriam Margolyes

What a load of . . .!

Here are some rhymes and jingles I made up. I made this one up looking out of the window of a bus, out of some of the things I saw and heard. It goes like this:

'Green tomato chutney'
'Fresh cottage cheese'
'Shop-along Bingo'
'All fares please'

Dustbins

Down behind the dustbin
I met a dog called Jim.
He didn't know me
and I didn't know him.

Down behind the dustbin
I met a dog called Felicity.
'It's a bit dark here,' she said.
'They've cut off the electricity.'

Down behind the dustbin
I met a dog called Jack.
'Are you going anywhere?' I said.
'No. I'm just coming back.'

Down behind the dustbin
I met a dog called Anne.
'I'm just off now,' she said,
'to see a dog about a man.'

Down behind the dustbin
I met a dog called Mary.
'I wish I wasn't a dog,' she said.
'I wish I was a canary.'

Say each one of these three times quickly

If he could sell her salt,
I could sell her a salt-cellar
for salt for her celery.

I watched a car-wash wash a car.
I wish I was washed like car-washes wash cars.

She said,
'Should she show
a soldier her shoulder?'

What's your name?

When they said,
'What's your name?'
I used to say,
'Michael Rosen.
Rosen
R,O,S,E,N
with a silent Q as in rhubarb.'

and they'd say,
'That's not very funny.'

Old Ben Brown

This ship in the dock was at the end of its trip.
The man on deck was the captain of the ship.
The name of the captain was Old Ben Brown.
He played the ukelele with his trousers down.

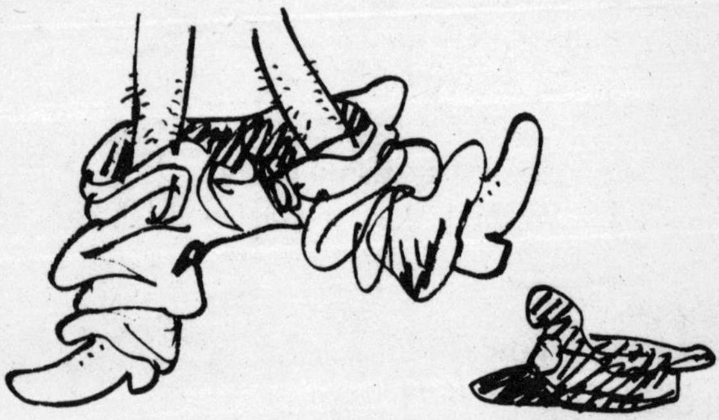

I saw a lady

I saw a lady with red hair
talking to one with blue on

the sun shone
and the rain ran
the streets emptied
the people had gone

when I looked
for the ladies again
there was a purple stream
flowing down the drain.

The Hidebehind

Have you seen the Hidebehind?
I don't think you will, mind you,
because every time you look for him
the Hidebehind's behind you.

Your brother Danny

Your brother Danny's got a golden nose,
and fish swim out of his eyes.
Your brother Danny's got legs like rhubarb,
and ears like apple pies.

Late last night

Late last night
I lay in bed
driving buses
in my head.

ME: 'Late last night
I lay in bed.'

GRAN: 'You lay in lead?'
ME: ' "In bed," I said.'

GRAN: 'You led your bed?'
ME: 'I said: "I lay".'

GRAN: 'You lay in bed?
You should have said.'

The man

The man on the corner
with broken glasses
sits on the bench
and watches who passes.

The hens of Never-when

The angry hens from Never-when
had a fight and lost their legs.
Now it's hot
where they squat
and they're laying soft-boiled eggs.

Ask no questions

Ask no questions
tell no lies.
Ever seen mincemeat
in mince pies?

Family-size pack

A little red alarm clock

I used to have a little red alarm clock.
It was my dad's.
He gave me it,
and I used to keep it by the side of my bed.

It was very small and it had legs
only the legs were like little balls –
little metal balls,
and you could unscrew them
out of the bottom of that little red clock.

One morning
I was lying in bed
and I was fiddling with my clock
and I unscrewed one of those
little ball-leg things
and, do you know what I did?
I slipped it into my mouth – to suck,
like a gob-stopper.

Well it was sitting there,
underneath my tongue
when I rolled over
and – ghulkh – I swallowed it:
the leg off my clock.
It had gone. It was inside me. A piece of metal.

I looked at the clock.
It was leaning over on its side.
I stood it up and of course it fell over.

So I got up,
went downstairs with it
and I was holding it out in front of me
and I walked into the kitchen
and I said:
'Look, the clock. The leg. The leg. The clock –
er . . .'

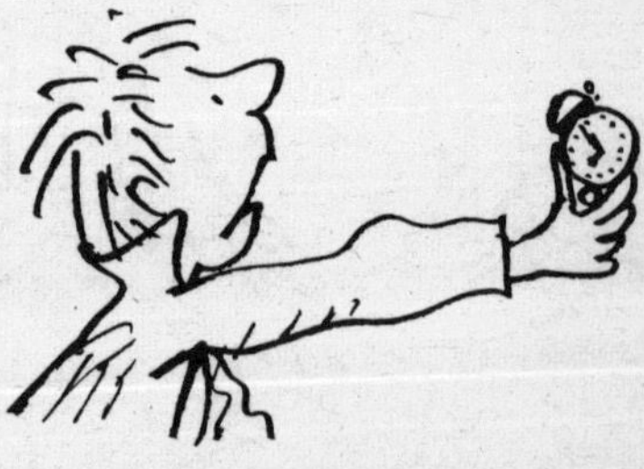

And my dad took it off me and he said,
'What's up, lad? Did you lose it?
Not to worry, it can't have gone far.
We'll find it and we can screw it back on in here,
look.'

'I swallowed it,' I said.

'You swallowed it? You swallowed it?
Are you mad? Are you stark staring mad?
You've ruined a perfectly good clock.
That was a good clock, that was. Idiot.
Now what's the use of a clock that won't stand
up?'
He held it out in front of him,
and he stared at it. I looked at it too.
I was wondering what was happening to the leg.

Grandad

When we go over
to my grandad's
he falls asleep.

While he's asleep
he snores.

When he wakes up,
he says,
'Did I snore?
did I snore?
did I snore?'

Everybody says, 'No,
you didn't snore.'

Why do we lie to him?

My dad's thumb

My dad's thumb
can stick pins in wood
without flinching –
it can crush family-size matchboxes
in one stroke
and lever off jam-jar lids without piercing
at the pierce here sign.

If it wanted
it could be a bath-plug
or a paint-scraper
a keyhole cover or a tap-tightener.

It's already a great nutcracker
and if it dressed up
it could easily pass
as a broad bean or a big toe.

In actual fact, it's quite simply
the world's fastest envelope burster.

I share my bedroom

I share my bedroom with my brother
and I don't like it.
His bed's by the window
under my map of England's railways
that has a hole in just above
  the town of Leicester
where Tony Sanders, he says,
killed a Roman soldier
with the Radio Times.

My bed's in the corner,
and the paint on the skirting board,
round the bottom of the wall,
wrinkles when I push it with my thumb
– which I do sometimes when I go to bed
sometimes when I wake up
but mostly on Sundays
when we stay in bed all morning.

That's when he makes pillow dens
under the blankets
so that only his left eye shows,
and when I go deep-bed coal-mining
for elastoplast spools
that I scatter with my feet
the night before,
and I jump on to his bed
shouting: 'eeyoueeyoueeyouee'
heaping pillows on his head:
'Now breathe, now breathe,'
and then there's quiet and silence
so I pull it away quick
and he's there laughing all over
sucking fresh air along his breathing-tube fingers.

Actually, sharing's all right.

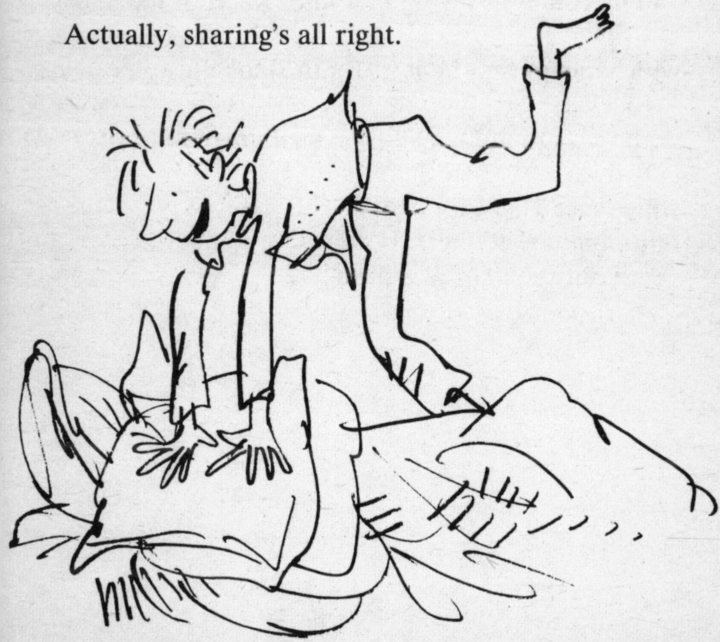

This morning

This morning my father looks out the window,
   rubs his nose
and says: Lets go and saw up logs
me and you.
So I put on my thick blue socks
and he puts on his army vest
and he keeps saying: Are you ready
   are you ready
It's a snorter of a day just look at the trees
and I run downstairs to get my old bent boots
that everybody says go round corners
   on their own they're so bent
and he comes in saying that his tobacco is like old
   straw
which means that he is going to smoke his pipe
   today
So he says to mum: We'll be back in an hour or
   two
which means not for ages
but mum doesn't hear, because we lumberjacks
   are out the door in a flash

Father says . . .

Father says
Never
let
me
see
you
doing
that
again
father says
tell you once
tell you a thousand times
come hell or high water
his finger drills my shoulder
never let me see you doing that again.

My brother knows all his little sayings
 off by heart
so we practise them in bed at night.

Wholemeal bread

My brother is making a fuss about bread.
'Why do we always have wholemeal bread?
You can't spread butter on wholemeal bread.
You try and spread the butter on
and it just makes a hole right through
the middle.'

He marches out of the room and shouts
across the landing and down the passage.
'It's always the same in this place.
Nothing works.
The volume knob's broken on the radio
you know.
It's been broken for months and months
you know.'

He stamps back into the kitchen
stares at the loaf of bread and says:
'Wholemeal bread – look at it, look at it.
You put the butter on
and it all rolls up.
you put the butter on
and it all rolls up.'

My brother gets letters

My brother gets letters – not many, but some,
I don't know why – but I get none.
Odd people seem to write to him –
a card to say his bike's done or a library book's in.
He seems to have friends, who when they're
  away
write about their holiday,
like – 'We're near the beach, had chips last night,
my bed squeaks and sand fleas bite.'
And sometimes he gets letters out of the blue
from people who can't know who they're writing to
offering him *The Reader's Digest Bird Book*
  cheap
or adverts for films like *The Blobs* – GIANT JELLIES
  THAT EAT AS THEY CREEP.
But I don't get anything. No one writes to me.
That is – until just recently.

You see I was looking at the paper one day,
and I was reading about this man's brain – it was
fading away.
That is – until he had done this Memory Course,
and discovered his Inner Mind Force.
And when you got down to the end
It said: 'This sounds GREAT – please send
to me at this address now:
*So You Want To Save Brain-Cells? – Here's
How.*'
And you filled in your name and address along
dotted lines
and sent it off to: Great Minds
P.O. Box 16, Manchester 8.
It was as simple as that. Sit and wait.

Now as it happens I wasn't very worried about
my Inner Mind Force
or the ones to cure baldness or put me on
a slimming course,
but the thing was – they all had something
for free
which they promised they'd send – addressed
to me.
What could be better?
I'd get a letter.
So after I'd got some of these forms together,
I came back then to my brother
and I said: 'I bet, out of us two,
I get more letters than you.'
And he said: 'Rubbish, no one ever writes
to you,
you're a Nobody, a No-one-knows-who.'
'Right,' I said, 'we'll keep a score,
me and you – see who gets more.'
'Great,' he said, and shook my hand. 'Done!
What do I get,' he said, 'when I've won?'
'No prizes,' I said. 'But whoever loses,
will have to do whatever the winner chooses.'
'Great,' he said again – and laughed,
he must have thought I was daft
to take him on.
He thought he couldn't go wrong.
'I'll show him,' I thought. 'What I can't wait
to see
is his face when these people write back to me.'

So anyway, I sent off about three or four
and soon I got what I was hoping for.
A former Mr Universe had written to say:
'BUILD POWER-PACKED MUSCLES
in just 70 seconds a day!!!'
'There you are,' I said to my brother.
'A letter – one nil – and tomorrow I'll be getting
another.'
So while he read what they had sent me
'Rippling muscles on guarantee
see your strength rise
right before your very eyes
on the built-in POWER-METER,'
I sat tight for my next letter.

Next to come through the post was
  Harvey Speke.
'I see my years of fatness as a past nightmare
  I'll never repeat.
Why be fat when you can be slim?
Shrink your waistline, stomach and chin,
I used to look like THIS – believe it or not!'
And there were pictures of bellies and heaven
  knows what
before and after shrinking with the Miracle Pill.
I didn't read the rest – 'Two nil!'
I said to my brother. 'I'm winning, aren't I?
You can't win now.' But he says: 'Oh can't I?'
and I can see he's getting really angry
reading about pills to stop you feeling hungry.

Next day there were two more –
one was a rather glossy brochure
on an Old Age Pension Plan,
and the other on Shoes For The Larger Man.
For three days he hadn't got anything through
the post.
He sat there at breakfast munching his toast
staring at his plate, while I was making a neat
stack
of leaflets and letters I'd got back.
'Four nil now, isn't it? Give in?
You see,' I said, 'every day I'm getting
something.'
And sure enough *something* arrived
not long after,
but it wasn't quite what *I* was after.

It was a great big parcel – it had come from
Liverpool.
'Who's it for?' I said. 'You, you fool.'
It was the first parcel I'd ever had in my life.
'Go on – open it,' father said, 'here's a knife.'
And they all stood round to see who'd sent
a parcel to me.
Even my brother wanted to see.
It was wrapped in red paper but the box was
brown.
I pulled the lid off – and it was an eiderdown.
'What is it?' 'A pillow?'
'Who sent it?' 'I don't know.'
'How much did it cost you?' 'What do you
mean?'

‘Don’t be funny – he hasn’t got a bean.’
I panicked. I came over cold.
Don’t forget – I was only nine years old.
‘Did you send off for this thing?’
‘No,’ I said. ‘All I did was fill a form thing in,
it said there was something for free –
fill in the form and it’d come to me.’
‘Fat-head! That means free till the seventh day,
keep it longer than that and you’ve got to pay.
Send it back if you don’t.
Mind you – I bet you won’t.’
‘Don’t say that,’ said mother. ‘He wasn’t to know better.’
‘But what was he doing?’ ‘I wanted a letter.’
‘Well get your friend Mart to send you cards from Wales when he goes
instead of sending off for boxes of bed-clothes.’

I felt such an idiot looking at the eiderdown.
I looked at my brother. He looked round.
'What's the matter? Five nil. Well done.'
He laughed. 'I think you've won,
or do you want to go on for a bit more?'
'No no no,' I said, 'I don't care about the score.'
'So you'll wrap up the box and send it back?'
father said.
'Unless you want to pay for a new eiderdown
on your bed.'
But I didn't do it straightaway,
and I didn't do it the next day,
or the next, or the next,
the eiderdown and the wrapping were in
a gigantic mess.

'The eiderdown's growing,' I was thinking.
'No! The box to send it back in's shrinking.'
Anyway fourth day on – eiderdown still not sent,
we were all having tea – the doorbell went.

My brother looks up. 'Probably the police –
on the hunt for an eiderdown thief.'
Father went to see who was there,
and we could hear voices from where we were.
Moment later – he's back – very long in the face.
He looks at me. 'It's for you,' he says.
I could have died. 'Is it the police
on the hunt for an eiderdown thief?'
'No,' he says, 'there's a man out there.
He's got something for you.' 'Out where?
Men don't come round here for me.'
But I went to the door and they all followed
to see.

'Mr Rosen, is it?' The man looked.
He was reading my name out of a black book.
'No,' I said. 'You want my father.'
'*M* Rosen?' he says. 'He's *H*, I gather.'
I said, 'Yes. I'm M.'
So he says, 'Good. Right then,
it's outside. Shall I wheel it in?'
'What?' I said. 'The washing machine.'
'Washing machine? Oh no. Not for me.'
'Well it says here "*M* Rosen", all right. Do you
want to see?'
'No,' I said, 'I only send for free things.'
'Yes, the demonstrations *are* free,' he says,
'but not the washing machines.'
'I don't want it.' I looked round for help.
You can imagine how I felt.
But they were hiding behind the door
laughing their heads off – my brother
on the floor.
I turned back. Looked up at the man.
'I've brought it now,' he says. 'It's in the van.'
'I've come all the way from Hoover's to show it
you.'
'No,' I said. 'No?' he said. 'Haven't you got
anyone else I could show it to?'
For a moment – it felt like a week –
he looked down at me – I looked down
at my feet.
Then he shut his book and went, and I shut
the door,
and straightaway my brother was there with
'Shall I add that to your score?

Six nil? Have you won yet?'
I said, 'I've had enough of this letter bet.'
And he said, 'Why? Don't you want a washing
  machine?
You could use it to keep your eiderdown clean!'
'Oh no! The eiderdown.' For a moment
  I'd forgotten about it.
'I can't get it in. The box – it's shrunk!'
  I shouted.
But mum said, 'I'll help you send that back,
  don't worry.
But what's coming next? A coat? A lorry?'
But father said, 'Who's won this bet?
And what's the winner going to get?'
My brother looked really happy and said,
  'I've lost –
Letters? *He's* the one that gets the most.'
'All I want,' I said, 'is I don't want to hear any
  more about it.
If I have to send off to get a letter – I'm better
  off without it.'
'OK,' my brother said, 'let's call it square.'
'Yes,' I said, 'we'll leave it there.'

But even now –
when there's someone asking for me at the door,
who mum has never seen before,
she says to me: 'It's for you, dear.
Quick! Your eiderdown's here!'

I'm the youngest in our house

I'm the youngest in our house
so it goes like this:

My brother comes in and says:
'Tell him to clear the fluff
out from under his bed.'
Mum says,
'Clear the fluff
out from under your bed.'
Father says,
'You heard what your mother said.'
'What?' I say.
'The fluff,' he says.
'Clear the fluff
out from under your bed.'
So I say,
'There's fluff under his bed, too,
you know.'
So father says,
'But we're talking about the fluff
under *your* bed.'
'You will clear it up
won't you?' Mum says.
So now my brother – all puffed up –
says,

'Clear the fluff
out from under your bed,
clear the fluff
out from under your bed.'
Now I'm angry. I am angry.
So I say – what shall I say?
I say,
'Shuttup Stinks
YOU CAN'T RULE MY LIFE.'

Out and about

Mart was my best friend

Mart was my best friend.
I thought he was great,
but one day he tried to do for me.

I had a hat – a woolly one
and I loved that hat.
It was warm and tight.
My mum had knitted it
and I wore it everywhere.

One day me and Mart were out
and we were standing at a bus-stop
and suddenly
he goes and grabs my hat
and chucked it over the wall.
He thought I was going to go in there
and get it out.
He thought he'd make me do that
because he knew I liked that hat so much
I wouldn't be able to stand being without it.

He was right –
I could hardly bear it.
I was really scared I'd never get it back.
But I never showed it on my face.
I just waited.

'Aren't you going to get your hat?'
he says.
'Your hat's gone,' he says.
'Your hat's over the wall.'
I looked the other way.
But I could still feel on my head
how he had pulled it off.
'Your hat's over the wall,' he says.
I didn't say a thing.

Then the bus came round the corner
at the end of the road.

If I go home without my hat
I'm going to walk through the door
and mum's going to say,
'Where's your hat?'
and if I say,
'It's over the wall.'
She's going to say,
'What's it doing there?'
and I'm going to say,
'Mart chucked it over.'
and she's going to say,
'Why didn't you go for it?'
and what am I going to say then?
what am I going to say then?

The bus was coming up.
'Aren't you going over for your hat?
There won't be another bus for ages,'
Mart says.

The bus was coming closer.
'You've lost your hat now,'
Mart says.

The bus stopped.
I got on.
Mart got on.
The bus moved off.

'You've lost your hat,' Mart says.
'You've lost your hat,' Mart says.

Two stops ahead, was ours.
'Are you going indoors without it?' Mart says.
I didn't say a thing.

The bus stopped.

Mart got up
and dashed downstairs.
He'd got off one stop early.
I got off when we got to our stop.

I went home
walked through the door
'Where's your hat?' Mum says.
'Over a wall,' I said.
'What's it doing there?' she says.
'Mart chucked it over there,' I said.
'But you haven't left it there, have you?' she says.
'Yes,' I said.

'Well don't you ever come asking me
to make you
anything like that again.
You make me tired, you do.'

Later,
I was drinking some orange juice.
The front door-bell rang.
It was Mart.
He had the hat in his hand.
He handed it to me – and went.

I shut the front door –
put on the hat
and walked into the kitchen.
Mum looked up.
'You don't need to wear your hat indoors
do you?'
she said.
'I will for a bit,' I said.
And I did.

My first love

A true story.

First love
when I was ten.

We planned a trip
up to town
Quite a grand thing to do
Up to town
The long ride on the train
all the way
up to town.

The day before our trip
up to town
She said, 'Do you mind if Helen
comes with us
up to town?'
'Great,' I said,
'all three of us, we'll all go
on the train
up to town.'

So that's how it was –
all three of us,
her, Helen and me
going on our trip
up to town.

But when we got
up to town,
all three of us –
her, Helen and me,

there was this long tunnel
and her friend, Helen,
goes and says:
'Hey – let's run away from him.'
And that's what they did.

So then there wasn't
all three of us any more.
There was just me,
standing in the tunnel.
I didn't chase after them.
I went home.

What's the matter?
or
How to do nothing and lose everything

Him and her. You can make your own mind up which is 'him' and which is 'her'.

What's the matter?
Nothing.
Something's the matter.
No, it isn't.
Then what are you sulking about?
I'm not sulking.
Well you're not exactly happy, are you?
I'm all right.
You don't look it.
I don't have to show it.
You used to.
So now I don't.
You're telling me.
Yes, I know I'm telling you.
Something's the matter then.
No, it isn't.
Yes, it is.
Well, if you know so much about me
  you don't need me to tell you.
No, I suppose not. I'll be off then. I'll see you
  when I see you.

What I did in town

I said:
I'll tell you what I did in town
I saw a greengrocer in the underground
with his pockets full of oranges,
a paperboy yawned
so you could see his tonsils,
there was one old football boot
lying in city square
and round the island came the Odeon
   commissionaire
riding on a moped with his uniform flying,
a hamster saw a parrot sneeze,
the shop blinds flapped and an oiltanker
   squealed,
the peanut man
lost a bag beneath a bus's wheels
'Mind your peanuts' a girl shouted,
his tray was slipping and a taxi hooted,
'O help me then' he called out
I said: 'where I'm sorry where?'
and forty thousand pigeons climbed into the air.

Views from the train

When you go on the train
and the line goes past the backs of houses
  in a town
you can see there's thousands and thousands
of things going on:
someone's washing up,
a baby's crying,
someone's shaving,
someone said, 'Rubbish, I blame
  the government.'
someone tickled a dog
someone looked out the window
and saw this train
and saw me looking at her
and she thought
'There's someone looking out the window
looking at me.'

But I'm only someone
looking out the window
looking at someone
looking out the window
looking at someone.

Then it's all gone.

Believe me – thousands wouldn't!

Do you know your eyes pop out?

Some people
are always passing comments.
They say to me:
hallo hairy
your hands are huge
do you know your eyes pop out?
you're a monster
you aren't half white
your fingers are like sausages
you walk like a bear
is that thing on your chin
a wart?

Bad habits

'Cigarette, Mike?' they say,
'I don't smoke,' I say.
'Haven't you got any bad habits?' they say.
'Yes,' I say, 'I chew bus tickets.'

I can't stop it.
The conductor gives me my ticket
and before I know I've done it
I've rolled it up
and I'm sucking on it like a cigarette.

I hold it with my fingers.
I roll it.
I flick it.
I hold it in my lips.

But there's a snag with my bus-ticket cigarettes:
they go soggy
they go gooey
and I nibble
and I bite
and I chew –
my bus tickets get shorter and shorter
and before I know I've done it
all I've got is a ball of soggy paper
rolling round my mouth.

Disgusting.

Smokers buy pills to stop their filthy habit.
All I've got is bus inspectors.

You see, once, not long ago,
I was on a bus,
and my ticket was in a ball
rolling round my mouth,
and suddenly – above me –
there's the inspector.
'Tickets, please,' he says
and there's me – nibble, nibble, nibble
on the mushed-up ball of paper in my mouth.

He wants to see my ticket.
Of course he can see my ticket
if he doesn't mind inspecting
a little ball of mush.

So I say, 'Yes, you can see my ticket.'
and I stuck my finger in my mouth
and hauled out the blob.

He looks at it.
He looks at me.
It's sitting there on the end of my finger.
'What's that?' he says,
'My ticket,' I said,
'What did you have for breakfast?' he says.
'Corn Flakes,' I said.
'Mmm,' he says,
'Did you ever think of having a slice or two
of toast,
as well, old son,' he says,
'and maybe you won't be so tempted by our
tickets.'
And he left it at that.

But it's very hard to break the habit,
even after a warning like that.
Got any ideas?

I've had this shirt

I've had this shirt
that's covered in dirt
for years and years and years.

It used to be red
but I wore it in bed
and it went grey
cos I wore it all day
for years and years and years.

The arms fell off
in the Monday wash
and you can see my vest
through the holes in the chest
for years and years and years.

As my shirt falls apart
I'll keep the bits
in a biscuit tin
on the mantelpiece
for years and years and years.

Today

Today was not
very warm
not very cold
not very dry
not very wet.

No one round here
went to the moon
or launched a ship
or danced in the street.

No one won a great race
or a big fight.

The crowds weren't out
the bands didn't play.

There were no flags no songs
no cakes no drums.
I didn't see any processions.
No one gave a speech.

Everyone thought today was ordinary,
busy busy
in out in
hum drummer day
dinner hurry
grind away day.

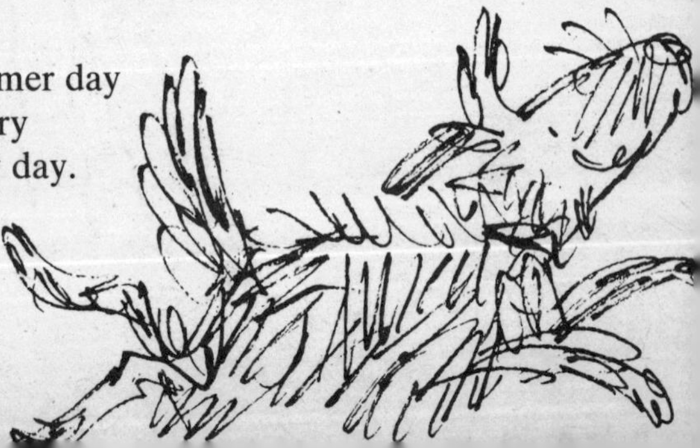

Nobody knows that today
was the most special day
that has ever ever been.

Ranzo, Reuben Ranzo,
who a week and a year ago was gone
lost
straying starving
under a bus? in the canal?
(the fireman didn't know)
was here, back,
sitting on the step
with his old tongue lolling,
his old eyes blinking.

I tell you –
I was so happy
So happy I tell you
I could have grown a tail –
and wagged it.

Loach

The best pet I ever had
was a fish I caught in a net.
It was three inches long
and it had six whiskers round its mouth.
I looked it up in a book
and they said it was called a loach,
not roach – loach.

I put it in a tank
but the tank was by the window
where the sun came in,
so the tank went green,
a very very dark green.
And no one believed
I had anything in there –
let alone anything called a loach.
They said: 'All you've got in there
is snails and old pond-weed.'

Sometimes I'd go and sit by the tank,
and look in.
And I wouldn't see anything at all.
But sometimes I'd go and sit by the tank
and my loach would suddenly
come to the wall of the tank
where I could see it,
and I'd watch it
push the glass wall
push its whiskers along the gravel on the bottom
and then go back into the dark green water
where I couldn't see it, any more.

But no one believed I had anything in there
because no one ever sat by the tank
long enough to see it.

I keep hearing things

Here is the news

In Manchester today a man was seen
with hair on top of his head.
Over now straightway to our Northern
  correspondent:
Hugh Snews.

'It's been a really incredible day
here in Manchester. Scenes like this
have been seen here every day
for years and years. It's now quite certain

no one will be saying anything about this
for months to come. One eyewitness said so.
"Are you sure?" I said.
She said: "No."
Back to you in London.'

All round the world,
newspapers, radio and television
have taken no notice of this story
and already a Prime Minister
has said nothing about it at all.

What next?
Rumour McRumourbungle,
Expert expert in expert experts?

'I doubt it. I doubt whether
anyone *will* doubt it – but I do.'

'What?'

'Doubt it.'

Thank you, Rumour McRumourbungle.
But how did it all begin?
As dawn broke in Manchester it soon became
   clear.
It's quite likely there was a lot of air in the air.
An hour after a few minutes had gone,
a couple of seconds passed
and a minute later at 12.15
it was a quarter past twelve.

Suddenly from across the other side of the road,
on the side facing this side,
there was the same road from the other side.
This side was now facing that side
and the road on that other side
was still opposite this.
Then – it happened.
There is no question of this.
In fact – no one has questioned it at all.
Further proof of this comes from the police
who say that a woman held for questioning
was released immediately
because she didn't know the answers
to the questions that no one asked her . . .
So –
it's something of a mystery.

Yes –
it's a mysterious thing to some
and there are some who think
it could
in a mysterious way
be nothing at all.

Here are the football results

League Division Fun
Manchester United won, Manchester City lost.
Crystal Palace 2, Buckingham Palace 1
Millwall Leeds nowhere
Wolves 8 A cheese roll and had a cup of tea 2
Aldershot 3 Buffalo Bill shot 2
Evertonill, Liverpool's not very well either
Newcastle's Heaven Sunderland's a very nice
place 2
Ipswhich one? You tell me.

I was going to see my Uncle Harry and I was standing on a station when I heard this announcement

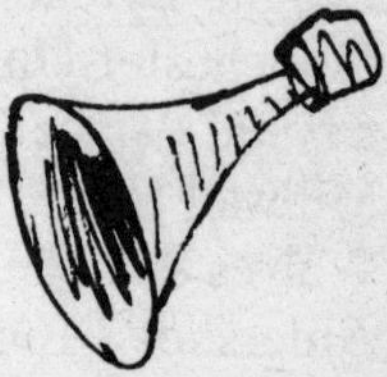

The train now standing
at Flatworm's heaven
will not stop or start
at Oldham, Newham
You bring 'em, We buy 'em,
and all stations to
Kahalacahoo, Hawaii.

All messengers for
Upshot, Caughtshort
Stick'em up and Hijack
should travel in the slow coaches
at the rear of the train.

All passengers with messages
for Uncle Harry's cabbages
should stake their seats
in quicker coaches
now that Uncle Harry's cabbages
need weeding out
and watering.

Problem page from a women's magazine

Dear Maureen,
I am a lamp-post.
Every Saturday evening at five o'clock
three boys
wearing blue and white scarves
blue and white hats
waving their arms in the air
and shouting,
come my way.
Sometimes they kick me.
Sometimes they kiss me.
What should I do
to get them to make up their minds?
Yours bewilderedly,
Annie Onlight.

There's more to this than meets the ear

Teachers – the inside story

Rodge said,
'Teachers – they want it all ways –
You're jumping up and down on a chair
or something
and they grab hold of you and say,
'Would you do that sort of thing in your own
  home?'

So you say, 'No.'
And they say,
'Well don't do it here then.'

But if you say, 'Yes, I do it at home.'
they say,
'Well, we don't want that sort of thing
going on here
thank you very much.'

'Teachers – they get you all ways,'
Rodge said.

The man said: 'When I die . . .'

A long time ago
there was a man who lived round our way
and he said:
'When I die,
I don't want to be buried in the ground
I want to be buried in the air.'
So he sat about making sure
he would be buried in the air.
He got people to build him a big yellow tower.
He said, 'I want to be buried halfway up
 this tower.'
Not long after, he died.
When they came to bury him,
they decided that they didn't want to bury him
in the air, halfway up the tower,
so they buried him in the ground instead
and there was nothing on earth he could do
 about it.
But the tower's still there
and everyone knows it was built for the man
who wanted to be buried in the air,
but couldn't make sure he would be.

A wasp in a wasp-trap talks

I am a wasp.
I am stuck in a sticky jar.
I used to fly in the wind
buzz my wings in the sun
and hover in sweet places

but I am stuck in a sticky jar.

Up I fly
and my wings hit a tin lid
my hard yellow head knocks it
so down I glide for a flicker of a second
   and my legs, my body
are in sweet water where there is no breath
   to breathe.

I used to soar and swoop.
I used to circle round and round
and settle on sweet things

but I am stuck in a sticky jar.

Above me the heat of the sun
pours through holes in the tin.
I buzz and crawl to them.
Isn't that the way I came in?
– but nearly there, my feelers
   hit tin.
The ragged cut edge of tin.
And who am I to dare to drag this weak waist
across that edge?

Beneath me, all about me,
is the smell of crushed strawberry.
It doesn't grow stronger if I buzz nearer.
It doesn't grow weak if I hover or move.
It's strong everywhere in smell
and nowhere to be found.

I used to *find* crushed strawberries –
or maybe melting chocolate, the hearts
   of fat plums.
I used to cut my way to the syrup
   of bruised bananas
in the gutters of the market.
I used to linger on the rims of glasses and bottles
to nibble at the crystals of lemonade, cherryade
and old orange pop.

All around me now
other wasps, even a bee and a blue-bottle
buzz up buzz down
and we're all swerving to miss each other's wings.

I turn back.
One is at my foot.
I twist to dodge him
but he is at my neck.
I snip at his scales –
he twists, a hairsbreadth from my eye.
A sting sticks, waves to find
a soft spot to get in.
I cut back, take off
and my wing is flying in the sweet water
dragging me down.

I use my legs and run up over the backs
of wasps floating where water and glass meet.
They sink. I sink.
And the buzz in the sweet smell of the air
goes on and on.
There is heat in the sun through the holes
in the lid of the tin.
The heat pours in.
Up above me, my eyes shadowy with the sugar
see a hole for the heat.

Into it come the eyes, the feelers, the jaws,
the head, the legs, the chest, the –

Those of us in here could say:
Go back.

But those of us in here who could say
are no more than black and yellow scum,
dead froth bobbing on the water.

In through the hole comes the chest,
the wings, the waist, the body and the sting.

Too late,
you silly, sugar-sniffing, soft nibbling,
  sweet-sucker.
That's the end.

Look

Look – said the boy
the scaffold-man at work
is like a spider on his net

No – said the scaffold-man
I'm just a fly
in the trap the spider set

The Bakerloo flea

Not long ago I was in a pub round the Elephant and Castle, and I got talking to a woman, an oldish woman. And we were talking about this and that, and she said she used to be a cleaner down the Underground. I didn't know, but it seems as if every night after the last tube, they switch the electric current off and teams of night-cleaners go through the underground, along the tunnels, cleaning up all the muck, rubbish, fag ends and stuff that we chuck on to the lines. They sweep out between the lines on one station, and then, in a gang of about six or seven, walk on to the next station along the lines in the tunnels.

Anyway this woman (I don't know her name), she says to me:

'Did you ever hear talk of the Bakerloo flea?'

'Bakerloo flea?' I said. 'No, no never.'

'Well,' she said, 'you know there are rats down there – down the underground? Hundreds of 'em. And the thing is,' she said, 'is that some of them have grown enormous. Huge great big things.'

'I've heard of them,' I said. 'Super Rats.'

‘Right,’ she says. ‘Now you tell me,’ she says, ‘what lives on rats? Fleas, right? Fleas. So – the bigger the rats the bigger the fleas. Stands to reason. These rats, they feed on all the old garbage that people throw down on the lines. It’s amazing what people throw away, you know.’

She told me, they found a steak down there once, lipstick, a bowler hat, beads, a box of eggs and hundreds and hundreds of sweets – especially maltesers and those balls of bubble gum you get out of slot machines.

Anyway, the rats eat these, get big, and it seems that one day they were working the Bakerloo Line – Elephant and Castle to Finchley Road – and just before Baker Street one of the women in the gang was looking ahead, and she screamed out:

‘Look – look – what’s that?’ Up in front was a great, grey, spikey thing with huge hairy legs and big jaws. It was as big as a big dog – bigger.

And the moment she screamed, it jumped away from them, making a sort of grating, scraping noise. Well, they were scared stiff. Scared stiff. But they had to finish the job, so they carried on up the line to Finchley Road. But they didn’t see it again that night or the next, or the next.

Some of them thought they'd imagined it, because it can get very spooky down there. They sing and shout a lot she told me, and tell saucy jokes, not fit for my ears.

Anyway, about a fortnight later, at the same place – just before Baker Street on the Bakerloo Line – suddenly one of them looks up and there it was again. A great, big, grey, spikey thing with long legs and big jaws.

'It's a flea, sure to God it's a flea,' one of them said.

The moment it heard this, again it jumped. Again, they heard this scraping, grating sound, and it disappeared down the tunnel – in the dark. They walked on, Baker Street, St John's Wood, Swiss Cottage, to Finchley Road. Nothing.

Anyway – this time they had a meeting. They decided it *was* a flea, a gigantic flea, and it must have grown up from a family of fleas that had lived for years and years growing bigger and bigger, sucking the blood of all the fat rats down there.

So they decided that it was time to tell one of the high-ups in London Transport, or they wouldn't go down there any more.

For a start off, no one'd believe them.

'Just a gang of women seeing things in the

dark,' the supervisor said.

Right! One of them had a bright idea. She said:

'I'll tell you what we'll do – we'll tell them that we're coming out on strike, and we'll tell the papers about the flea, the Bakerloo flea. It'll be a huge scandal – no one'll dare go by tube, it'll be a national scandal.'

So they threatened the manager with this, and this time the high-ups really moved. They were so scared the story might get out, and they'd be blamed, and one of *them* would lose their jobs.

So for a start they stopped all cleaning on the Bakerloo Line, and one of the high-ups went down the tunnel with the women. You can just see it, can't you? Four in the morning, a gang of six women with feather dusters, and one of the bowler hat and briefcase brigade walking down the tunnel on the hunt for the Bakerloo flea. Sounded incredible to me.

Anyway, it seems as if they came round that same corner just before Baker Street and the women had gone quiet and the bloke was saying: 'If this is a hoax, if this is a trick . . .' when they heard that awful, hollow, scraping noise.

At first they couldn't see it, but then – there

it was – not *between* the lines this time – *on* the lines – a gigantic flea. No question, that's what it was.

Well, he took one look at it, and next moment he was backing off.

'Back, ladies, back. Back, ladies!'

Of course *he* was more scared than *they* were. Terrified. But he was even more terrified when one of the women let out this scream. Not because *she* was scared, but to scare off the flea. And it worked. It jumped. Right out of sight.

Well there was no carrying on up the line that night.

'Back, ladies, back,' was all he could say, and back they went.

Next thing they knew, they were all called into an office with a carpet and the Queen on the wall. And there was a whole gang of these men.

First thing, one of them says, they weren't to let anyone know of this, no one at all must ever hear of what they had all seen. There was no point in letting a panic develop. Anyway, next he says:

'We haven't let the grass grow under our feet. We've got a scientist with us.'

And then the scientist, he says:

'I've got this powder. Deadly flea powder. All you need to do is spread this up and down the Bakerloo Line, and there'll be no more trouble with this flea thing.'

Well, the woman in the pub – I never found out her name – said:

'So who's going to spread this stuff about down there? The Army?'

'No,' the man said. 'We don't see any need for that. You,' he says, 'you.'

'So that's a fine one,' the woman said to me. 'First of all they said it was just a bunch of women afraid of the dark, then they send Tarzan in pinstripes down there and he can't get out fast enough, and now it's us that had to spread this flea powder.'

'Well,' she said, 'we knew it wouldn't be any good anyway. Flea powder never is.'

They took it down there, threw it about between Regents Park and Baker Street and Swiss Cottage – while up above, in the big houses, ambassadors from all over the world slept soundly in their beds. They told them not to go down for a week, and not to breathe a word of it to anyone.

'They were more scared of a story in the papers than we were of the flea,' she said.

It hadn't attacked anyone, no one had seen it there in day time, so down they went. But there it was again – sitting there just before Baker Street, with some of the powder sticking to the hairs on its legs. But this time, instead of hopping away down the line, it turned and faced them. They turned and ran, and then it leaped. It leaped at the women, and they ran back down the tunnel to Regents Park. This great, grey flea was trying to get at them.

'We screamed,' she said, 'we really screamed, but it was after us, 'cos you see that damned flea powder hadn't killed the flea – it had killed the rats. It was starving for fresh blood. Probably *mad* for blood, by now,' she said. 'We ran and ran and the flea was hopping – but it was hitting the roof of the tunnel, it was so mad to get at us. There was this terrible scraping sound of its shell on the roof of the tunnel, and it'd fall back on to the lines. So we could move faster than it. We rushed back to Regents Park, and calls went up and down the line and all over the system to lock the gates on every station and seal the system. Seal off the underground system of London. Well, it was about four o'clock – two hours to go before a million people would be down there.

'What were they going to do? Upstairs in the office they were in a blind panic. They could've done something about it earlier, instead of fobbing us off. They couldn't call in the Army without telling the Minister, and if they told the Minister, he'd tell the Prime Minister, and all the high-ups would get the sack. So they had this plan to turn the current on, and run the maintenance train at high speed through the tunnel from Finchley Road to the Elephant and Castle, in the hope that it would get killed beneath the wheels of the train, or smashed against the buffers at the Elephant.

'They did it. They sent it through. Of course *that* didn't work. We knew it wouldn't work. Anyone that's lived with a flea knows you can't squash fleas – you've got to crack 'em. They're hard, rock hard.

'After the maintenance man ran the maintenance train through, they went down to the gates at Regents Park, and they stood and listened, and from down below they could hear the grating, scraping noise of its shell on its legs. Of course, it was obvious now why it had stuck to this stretch of the line all the time. Some of the juiciest rubbish was in the bins round those posh parts, so you got the biggest rats, so that was where you got the great Bakerloo flea.

'So now they had less than two hours to get

rid of the flea, or leave it for a day and run the risk of letting a million people down into the tunnels to face a flea, starving, starving for blood, or shutting the whole system down and telling everyone to go by bus.

'Well you know what happened?' she said. '*We* did it. *We* got rid of it.'

'You did?'

'Yes, we did it.

'Vera's old man worked on the dustcarts for Camden Council. She knew how to kill the flea. It was Vera's plan that what we'd do was go down, actually down onto the line at Oxford Circus with dustbin lids, banging them with brushes and broom handles, and drive the flea back up the line to Finchley Road where the Bakerloo Line comes out of the tunnel into the open air. And at Finchley Road, Vera's old man and his gang would have a couple of carts backed up into the tunnel. And that's what we did. We got driven to Vera's place to get her old man up, on to his mates' places to get them up, then they went to the Council builder's yard to get boards, builders' planks. We got the lids off the bins, and down we went. Oxford Circus, Regents Park, Baker Street, St John's Wood, Swiss Cottage, Finchley Road, and we shouted and we banged, and we banged and we shouted every step of the way.

'We saw it just once at Swiss Cottage waiting for us, but we walked together holding the lids up in front of us like shields, and it was as if it knew it couldn't get at us this time, 'cos it turned – it had just room to turn in the tunnel – and as we came up to Finchley Road still banging and shouting, it leaped – not at us, but at one of the carts. Alongside it was the other one, between the wheels were the boards, some of them stacked up to block off all the gaps. The flea was trapped between us with our lids and the back of the dustcarts. It leaped, it hit the roof of the tunnel, just like it did when it chased us. We shouted and banged. It leaped again. This time we had it. It was in the back of the dustcart. We kept up the banging and the shouting. We got as near to the back of the dustcart as we could. We could see it there, every hair of its legs, and Vera shouts:

' "Turn it on, Bob, turn it on", and Bob turned on the masher (they call it "The Shark"), in the back of his cart. And it bit into the back of that flea like giant nails crunching through eggshells. The smell was revolting. Bit by bit, the flea was dragged into the cart. We could see it as it went: first its body, then its legs. I'll never forget the sight of those huge hairy legs twitching about in the back of Bob's cart, Vera shouting:

' "You've got him, love, you've got him!"

'He had, too. That was that. That was the end of the Bakerloo flea. But do you know, when we got up to the top, that load from head office were there. They were crying, crying out of relief, crying their eyes out. Twenty minutes later, hundreds and thousands of people were down there, off to work, none the wiser. They didn't know about any flea, any Bakerloo flea. They don't even know we go down there every night cleaning up their mess for them. Of course, head office made us promise never to breathe a word of it. We promised.

'Vera said:

' "What's it worth to you?"

'He said:

' "Your honour. Your word. And your word's your honour."

'And they gave us a week's extra holiday tagged on to August Bank Holiday that year.'

She told me I was the first person she'd ever told the story to, and told me never to tell anyone. The scandal would be terrible. I don't know whether to believe her or not.

Index

Acknowledgements

We are grateful to the following for permission to reprint and record copyright material:
André Deutsch Ltd for reprint of poems 'I've had this shirt', 'This morning', 'What I did in town', 'Wholemeal bread' and for reprint and record of poems 'My dad's thumb', 'Dustbins', 'Old Ben Brown', 'I saw a lady', 'I share my bedroom' (slightly adapted), 'Father says . . .', 'The Hidebehind' (slightly adapted) from *Mind Your Own Business* by Michael Rosen (1974) and reprint of poems 'The man', 'Late last night', 'Your brother Danny', 'Ask no questions', 'Problem page from a women's magazine', 'Today' and reprint and record of poems 'My brother gets letters', 'I'm the youngest in our house', 'I was going to see my Uncle Harry . . .', 'A wasp in a wasp-trap talks', 'The hens of Never-when', 'Here is the news', 'Look' from *Wouldn't You Like To Know* by Michael Rosen (1977); English Centre for reprint and record of adapted version of story 'The Bakerloo Flea' by Michael Rosen. This story first appeared in *Teachers Writing* published by the ILEA English Centre; Penguin Books Ltd for reprint of poems 'Down behind the dustbin', 'Grandad' ('When we go over to my Grandad's'), 'Mart was my best friend', 'Do you know your eyes pop out' ('Some people are always passing comments'), 'Teachers – the inside story' ('Rodge said'), 'The man said . . .' ('A long time ago'), and reprint and record of poems 'Say each of these three times quickly' ('Three Tongue Twisters'), 'What's your name?' 'My first love' ('A true story'), 'Bad habits' ('A Bad Habit'), 'Here are the football results' ('You Tell Me'), 'A little red alarm clock' ('I used to have a little red alarm clock') by Michael Rosen from *You Tell Me*. Poems by Roger McGough and Michael Rosen (Kestrel Books, 1979) © 1979 by Michael Rosen. Reprinted by permission of Penguin Books Ltd; the author, Michael Rosen for 'What's the matter', 'Views from the train' and 'Loach'.

The titles of the poems in parentheses are as they appear in the Penguin publication.